FOND DU LAC PUBLIC LIBRARY
WITHDRAWN

World Religions

JUDAISM

by Elizabeth Andrews

WELCOME TO DiscoverRoo!

This book is filled with videos, puzzles, games, and more! Scan the QR codes* while you read, or visit the website below to make this book pop.

popbooksonline.com/judaism

abdobooks.com

Published by Pop!, a division of ABDO, PO Box 398166, Minneapolis, Minnesota 55439. Copyright © 2024 by Abdo Consulting Group, Inc. International copyrights reserved in all countries. No part of this book may be reproduced in any form without written permission from the publisher. DiscoverRoo™ is a trademark and logo of Pop!.

Printed in the United States of America, North Mankato, Minnesota.

052023
082023

THIS BOOK CONTAINS RECYCLED MATERIALS

Cover Photo: Shutterstock Images
Interior Photos: Shutterstock Images, Getty Images, Wikimedia Commons, Historia/Shutterstock
Editor: Tyler Gieseke
Series Designer: Laura Graphenteen

Library of Congress Control Number: 2022950564

Publisher's Cataloging-in-Publication Data
Names: Andrews, Elizabeth, author.
Title: Judaism / by Elizabeth Andrews
Description: Minneapolis, Minnesota : Pop!, 2024 | Series: World religions | Includes online resources and index
Identifiers: ISBN 9781098244477 (lib. bdg.) | ISBN 9781098245177 (ebook)
Subjects: LCSH: Judaism--Doctrines--Juvenile literature. | Judaism and culture--Juvenile literature. | World religions--Juvenile literature. | Religious belief--Juvenile literature.
Classification: DDC 296--dc23

*Scanning QR codes requires a web-enabled smart device with a QR code reader app and a camera.

TABLE OF CONTENTS

CHAPTER 1
Early Judaism 4

CHAPTER 2
The Torah and Practices 10

CHAPTER 3
Modern Jews 16

CHAPTER 4
Holidays and Celebrations 22

Making Connections 30
Glossary 31
Index 32
Online Resources 32

CHAPTER 1
EARLY JUDAISM

Judaism is the world's first religion to **worship** one God. It began more than 4,000 years ago. Judaism is a special religion because it includes more than just Jewish faith. It is the culture, history, and **heritage** of the Jewish people as well.

WATCH A VIDEO HERE!

The history of Judaism involves a lot of travel.

Thousands of years ago, God gave a man named Abraham a message. Abraham was told to take his family to the land of Canaan. If they obeyed, God promised to make Abraham and his **descendants** into a great nation. Abraham trusted God and obeyed.

Abraham and his descendants were God's chosen people. They were the first of the Jewish people. They grew into a large group called the Israelites.

Hundreds of years later, the Israelites traveled to Egypt. A pharaoh enslaved them because he saw their large numbers as a threat. They were enslaved for 400 years.

ABRAHAM AND ISAAC

Abraham had a son named Isaac. As a test of Abraham's faith, God told him to sacrifice Isaac. Abraham prepared for the sacrifice. God saw that Abraham fully trusted and had faith in Him. Because of Abraham's trust, God spared Isaac before the sacrifice could happen.

Abraham is the father of all Abrahamic religions. These include Judaism, Christianity, and Islam.

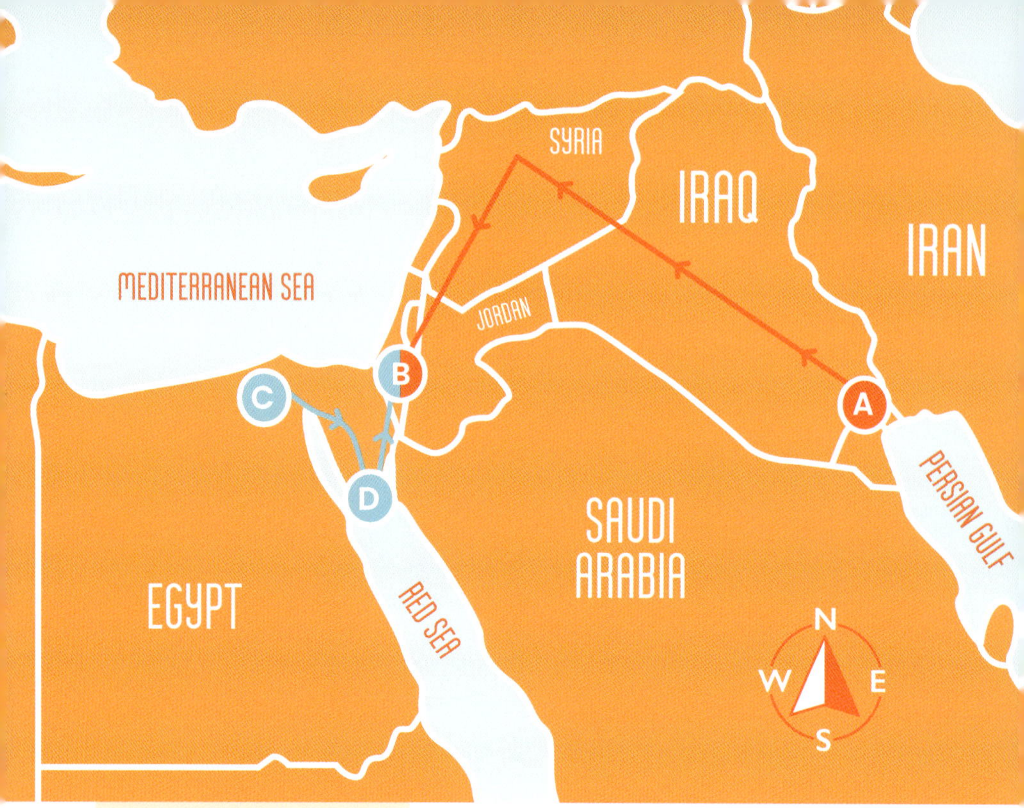

KEY

ABRAHAM'S PATH

 Ur

 Canaan

MOSES'S PATH

 Home of the Pharaoh

 Mount Sinai

 Canaan

MASS MOVEMENTS OF JEWS

The Jewish people moved around a lot in search of their homeland. When Abraham received God's message, he lived in Ur, a city of ancient Mesopotamia. He took his people to Canaan. Another time of mass movement was when Moses led the Israelites out of Egypt. Forced movement continued throughout Jewish history.

God chose a man named Moses to be his prophet and save the Israelites from slavery. Moses helped the Israelites escape to Mount Sinai. There, God gave more of His message and the Ten Commandments to Moses. God's messages to Abraham and Moses make up the Jewish Bible called the Torah.

Over time, Israelites became known as Jews. They were often controlled by outside forces. Jews went through periods of **exile**, wars, **genocide**, and slavery. The ability to survive struggle became a big part of Judaism.

DID YOU KNOW? Jewish people capitalize God's pronouns when referring to Him.

CHAPTER 2
THE TORAH AND PRACTICES

Jewish people believe that God is the creator and ruler of all things. He is everywhere and knows everything. They pray to speak with Him. God reveals His laws and guidance through prophets like Abraham and Moses.

LEARN MORE HERE!

The Ten Commandments are rules from God. They appeared to Moses written on a stone tablet.

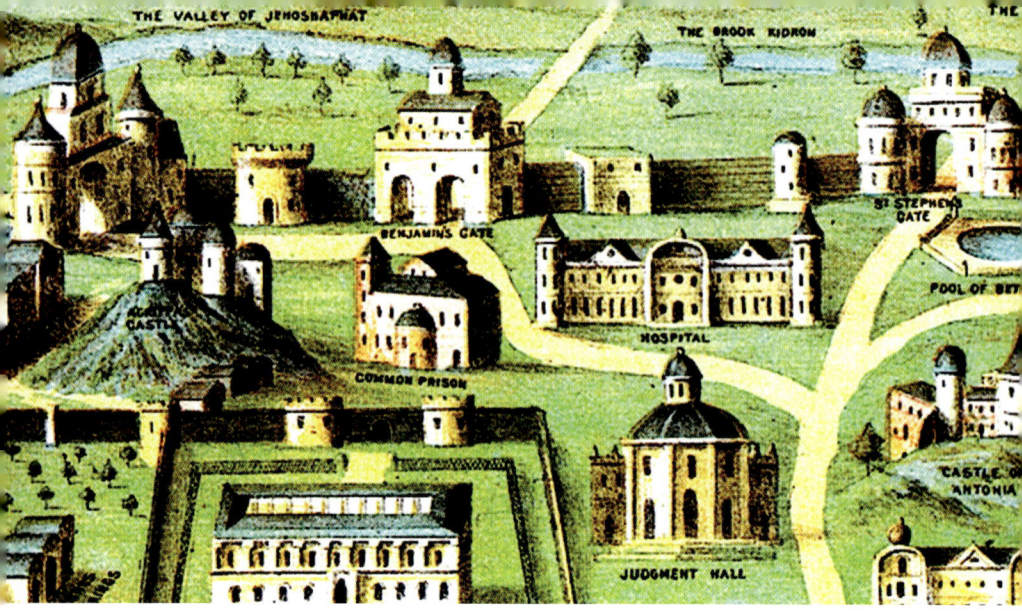

The Torah is the word of God. It is one part of the Hebrew Bible known as the Tanakh. The book lays out the beliefs and practices Jews follow. It teaches that all human life has an important purpose and tells Jews to be fair and just.

Early in Jewish history, Jews **worshipped** God at the Temple

A man named King Solomon built the First Temple in 957 BCE. It was in the holy city of Jerusalem.

of Jerusalem. Enemies of the Jews destroyed the First Temple. Then, they destroyed the Second Temple after it was built. Jews learned they could worship God anywhere. Synagogues are located all over the world. In these places of worship, Jews study scripture, pray, and spend time with their community.

Some synagogues are extravagantly decorated.

God made two covenants with the Jewish people. A covenant is when two partners love, care for, and stay loyal to one another. The first covenant was God's promise to Abraham before he left for Canaan. The second was between God and the Israelites when Moses received the Ten Commandments.

The second covenant says that if Jews live to serve God, they will get His blessings. Serving God includes praying to Him, treating people kindly, and following the rules He gave Moses.

The Ark of the Covenant was a chest covered in gold. The Ark was said to hold the stone tablet with the Ten Commandments.

CHAPTER 3
MODERN JEWS

There are different ways to follow Judaism. Orthodox Jews believe the faith should be practiced exactly as God told Moses. Some Orthodox Jews wear head coverings and follow strict rules about what food to eat. Men and women do not pray together in synagogues.

EXPLORE LINKS HERE!

The Star of David is a six-pointed star. It's used as decoration by many Jewish people and at synagogues. It symbolizes a shield of protection by God.

DID YOU KNOW? Some Jews believe God will send a person to lead the Jewish people to a new time of peace.

Reform Judaism began in the 1800s. These Jews took the religion and blended it with modern society. People wanted freedom and equality. Jewish **worship** began to include music. Men and women could be together in synagogues.

Braided challah bread is often eaten on the Sabbath. It is the holy day of rest lasting from sunset Friday until Saturday night.

The fur hat sometimes worn by married Jewish men is called a shtreimel.

Conservative Judaism honors tradition and modern life. There is some freedom and flexibility in its practice. Some Jewish people do not practice the religion at all. They are simply of Jewish **heritage**. They are still considered Jews. They feel connected to the people and their history.

Unfortunately, many non-Jews have not liked the Jewish religion or its people. From 1933 to 1945, more than six million Jewish people were killed by the German **Nazi** government. This **genocide** became known as the Holocaust. It ended when Germany lost World War II.

Events like the enslavement by Egyptians and the Holocaust connect all Jewish people to suffering. Jews who don't practice the religion can still connect with the suffering their people have faced.

During the Holocaust, Jewish people were also imprisoned in terrible places called concentration camps.

CHAPTER 4

HOLIDAYS AND CELEBRATIONS

Judaism is not just about suffering. There are several important holidays in Judaism filled with celebration. The celebrations honor God and the Jewish people's strength.

COMPLETE AN ACTIVITY HERE!

Challah is a sweet egg bread that is pulled apart to eat.

Many Jews wear shawls or head coverings in synagogues.

A shofar is blown at the beginning of Rosh Hashanah and at the end of Yom Kippur.

Rosh Hashanah is the ten-day Jewish New Year. Jews spend the days **repenting**. It starts on the first of Tishri. This is the seventh month of the Jewish calendar. Jewish New Year ends with the holiest day in Judaism, Yom Kippur. Jews spend 25 hours not eating and praying to God for forgiveness.

During Rosh Hashanah, Jews eat honey and apples in hopes of a sweet year ahead.

 **DID YOU KNOW?** There is a special Jewish calendar that does not follow the New Age calendar generally used.

Passover is a seven-day holiday. It honors the Jews' escape from Egypt. Seder is a special meal that takes place on the first two nights of Passover. Seders are joyous celebrations that have special foods, songs, and prayers. Most importantly, Jews read the biblical story of Exodus.

Rabbis are Jewish teachers and leaders.

In the story of Exodus, Israelites brushed sheep's blood over their doors to protect themselves from God's anger.

The bar mitzvah and bat mitzvah are symbolic holidays to welcome Jewish boys and girls into adulthood. The young person reads from the Torah at a

A synagogue has a Torah ark where the Torah scrolls are kept.

synagogue. Some families have parties after the ceremony to celebrate.

Jews will eat three delicious meals during the holy day of Sabbath. At a synagogue, a rabbi performs a ritual involving the Torah. Rabbis and other synagogue members read from the Torah. Then, the scrolls are returned to the ark.

The ancient religion of Judaism has changed the world. Many other religions owe their beginnings to Judaism.

A Torah scroll is a handwritten copy of the Torah.

MAKING CONNECTIONS

TEXT-TO-SELF

What person of Jewish history are you most interested in? Explain your answer.

TEXT-TO-TEXT

Have you read books about any other religions? If so, how were those religions similar to or different from Judaism?

TEXT-TO-WORLD

Jewish people spent a lot of their history traveling between places. Why do you think it was important to them to find and settle in a homeland?

GLOSSARY

descendant — a person born in a direct biological line. A person's children and grandchildren are their descendants.

exile — a period of forced absence from one's country or home.

genocide — the purposeful attempt to kill all members of a certain group of people.

heritage — something that one believes, thinks, or does that is handed down from their family background.

Nazi — a member of a political party that controlled Germany under Adolf Hitler from 1933 to 1945.

repent — to feel sorry for sins and work to avoid the same behavior moving forward.

sacrifice — to kill a person or animal as an offering to God.

symbolize — to serve as a symbol. A symbol is an object or mark that stands for something else.

worship — love and respect shown to God.

INDEX

Abraham, 6–10, 14

Canaan, 6, 8, 14

covenant, 14–15

Egypt, 7, 21, 26

God, 4, 6–10, 12–16, 22, 25

Hebrew Bible, 9, 12, 28–29

history, 4, 6–9, 12–15, 21

Holocaust, 21

Israelites, 6, 8–9, 14

Moses, 8–10, 14–16

Passover, 26

Rosh Hashanah, 25

synagogue, 13, 16, 18, 29

temple, 12–13

types of Judaism, 16, 18–19

Yom Kippur, 25

DiscoverRoo!
ONLINE RESOURCES

This book is filled with videos, puzzles, games, and more! Scan the QR codes* while you read, or visit the website below to make this book pop.

popbooksonline.com/judaism

*Scanning QR codes requires a web-enabled smart device with a QR code reader app and a camera.